EXISTENTIALISM

EXISTENTIALISM

BY
JEAN-PAUL SARTRE

Translated by Bernard Frechtman

PHILOSOPHICAL LIBRARY
NEW YORK

INTRODUCTION

THE VOGUE in America of Jean-Paul Sartre and his philosophy of existential- ism is one of those curious phenomena which might, if properly examined, illuminate some peculiarities of culture in America. Since the liberation of France, when reports on life during the occupation began to appear in this country, Sartre and his work have been the subject of curiosity and even of a formless kind of debate. This, despite the fact that none of his philosophical writings has hitherto appeared in English. Even the question of his originality has been raised. The daily press and the popu- lar magazines have reported on his personality and private life, on the supposed furor and scandal that attend his lectures and the open- ings of his plays, and even, in a casual way, on his ideas; the general impression given is a journalistic conception of an erratic left-bank bohemianism.

Three or four essays of Sartre have recently

appeared in literary magazines and so have made something available to a more serious kind of inquiry, though none of these papers is specifically philosophical, dealing as they do with contemporary French literature and with anti-Semitism. Selections from his novel, *Nausea*, have appeared in translation in Partisan Review, and his play *No Exit* was produced in New York at the end of 1946, but failed to run for more than a few weeks. All of this is far from adding up to anything that should give rise to a cogent discussion of a formal philosophy.

Yet, though the awareness that there is a Sartre and a French existentialism is for the most part on the level of gossip, the curiosity derives from another source. For something has emanated from the mélange of news articles and scattered pieces with a tonality of urgency; people have obscurely sensed that Sartre is occupied with a philosophy that is immediately involved in the peculiar confusions that beset this generation in all aspects of its civilization, the private as well as the public.

The present work is the first sustained exposition of Sartre's philosophy to appear in English. Originally a lecture delivered in Paris in 1945, it was later published, without alteration, as *L'Existentialisme est un humanisme*. The discussion which follows the essay is an exact transcription of the discussion which followed the lecture. M. Naville, who offers the most extended objections, is a well known French Marxist.

The chief effort of Sartre in this short work is to face squarely the implications for personal action of a universe without purpose. Assuming the non-existence of God, and denying the existence of a fixed human nature, Sartre refuses to allow man any support external to himself. He attacks evolutionary philosophies of history, particularly Marxism, because they obscure the fact that man is fully responsible for his nature and his choices. It is precisely the idea of man's personal responsibility for what he is and does that is at the heart of Sartre's argument. There are no values external to man and no given human nature which he is obliged to fulfill. Man chooses his values and makes himself, and for this choice he is responsible. But, in Sartre's view, this need not lead to quietism or despair. On the contrary, this awareness illuminates the needless burden that man carries and tries to force him to recognize that he is actively carrying it, rather than is passively impelled by it, that he may choose different values and may choose to be a different person. It tries to make man acutely aware of his freedom. And since freedom is an ambiguous state, both sought and feared, this philosophy is both frightening and liberating.

The question of the originality of Sartre's doctrines has been raised, and sometimes in such a way as to imply that their value is involved in the answer. It is unnecessary in this place to inquire into whatever may be its origins in the work of Heidegger, Kierkegaard, and others. A philosophy may achieve originality as poetry does, in its tone and language, as well as in its concepts. The specific linguistic quality of this brief work is inextricable from its full meaning and gives it its sharp quality of immediacy. It invokes the sense of concrete persons and objects and of the urgency of whatever action the philosophy demands. Its full

INTRODUCTION

meaning and weight appear not only in what
may be paraphrased, but, as in a poem, in the
emotional and visual landscape that is imminent in its language.

The character of Sartre's style has created a
peculiar problem of translation. The author is
both a man of the library and a man of the
streets and writes as such. A former teacher of
philosophy and the author of several formal
philosophical works, he is even more widely
known in France as a dramatist and novelist.
No one familiar with his literary writings can
fail to be struck with Sartre's knowledge of and
sensitivity to a wide and varied range of Pari-
sian life, including areas not usually regarded
as the preserve of the scholar. Yet nowhere is
there affectation. What we feel, regardless of
the logical validity of the philosophical writings, is that the philosophy exists in and through
a world of concrete circumstances, that it has
the alert quality of the perception of individual
life in motion, that it is, to use one of Sartre's
key words, involved in action. This quality is
the very life of the style of the present essay.
The sentences are nervous, even when pro-

tracted; the colloquial tone is general and, when not actually present, imminent. The matter on hand may, at a certain moment, be technical, but there is always the sense of its issuing from a man's sensibility and not a book.

I have attempted to render this quality without sacrificing the integrity of the thought. At times a certain obscurity may appear, but, without attempting to excuse whatever imperfections there may be in my rendering, I should like to remind the reader that the original text is that of a lecture and that it is evident that there are places where gestures and intonations probably conveyed nuances that are absent from the written text, but which it requires. I have not felt that it was within the scope of my duty as translator to allow my imagination to exceed the original text.

In the case of the transcribed discussion there is a looseness that is to be expected in impromptu remarks. The ideas stand out clearly enough, but they labor and ramble through language that is often inadequate to the complexity of the ideas. One feels the effort to express niceties of thought without the oppor-

tunity for composition particularly required by
an abstruse subject. I have not tried to polish
the crude surface of this discussion. Perhaps
readers will even find it not disagreeable.

B. F.

EXISTENTIALISM

I SHOULD LIKE on this occasion to defend existentialism against some charges which have been brought against it.

First, it has been charged with inviting people to remain in a kind of desperate quietism because, since no solutions are possible, we should have to consider action in this world as quite impossible. We should then end up in a philosophy of contemplation; and since contemplation is a luxury, we come in the end to a bourgeois philosophy. The communists in particular have made these charges.

On the other hand, we have been charged with dwelling on human degradation, with pointing up everywhere the sordid, shady, and slimy, and neglecting the gracious and beautiful, the bright side of human nature; for example, according to Mlle. Mercier, a Catholic critic, with forgetting the smile of the child. Both sides charge us with having ignored human solidarity, with considering man as an isolated being. The communists say that the main reason for this is that we take pure subjectivity, the *Cartesian I think,* as our starting point; in other words, the moment in which man becomes fully aware of what it means to him to be an isolated being; as a result, we are unable to return to a state of solidarity with the men who are not ourselves, a state which we can never reach in the *cogito.*

From the Christian standpoint, we are charged with denying the reality and seriousness of human undertakings, since, if we reject God's commandments and the eternal verities, there no longer remains anything but pure caprice, with everyone permitted to do as he pleases and incapable, from his own point of view, of condemning the points of view and acts of others.

I shall try today to answer these different charges. Many people are going to be surprised at what is said here about humanism. We shall try to see in what sense it is to be understood. In any case, what can be said from the very beginning is that by existentialism we mean a doctrine which makes human life possible and, in addition, declares that every truth and every action implies a human setting and a human subjectivity.

As is generally known, the basic charge

against us is that we put the emphasis on the dark side of human life. Someone recently told me of a lady who, when she let slip a vulgar word in a moment of irritation, excused herself by saying, "I guess I'm becoming an existentialist." Consequently, existentialism is regarded as something ugly; that is why we are said to be naturalists; and if we are, it is rather surprising that in this day and age we cause so much more alarm and scandal than does naturalism, properly so called. The kind of person who can take in his stride such a novel as Zola's *The Earth* is disgusted as soon as he starts reading an existentialist novel; the kind of person who is resigned to the wisdom of the ages—which is pretty sad—finds us even sadder. Yet, what can be more disillusioning than saying "true charity begins at home" or "a scoundrel will always return evil for good?"

We know the commonplace remarks made when this subject comes up, remarks which always add up to the same thing: we shouldn't struggle against the powers-that-be; we shouldn't resist authority; we shouldn't try to rise above our station; any action which doesn't conform to authority is romantic; any effort not based on past experience is doomed to failure; experience shows that man's bent is always toward trouble, that there must be a strong hand to hold him in check, if not, there will be anarchy. There are still people who go on mumbling these melancholy old saws, the people who say, "It's only human!" whenever a more or less repugnant act is pointed out to them, the people who glut themselves on *chansons réalistes;* these are the people who accuse existentialism of being too gloomy, and to such an extent that I wonder whether they are complaining about it, not for its pessimism, but much rather its optimism. Can it be that what really scares them in the doctrine I shall try to present here is that it leaves to man a possibility of choice? To answer this question, we must re-examine it on a strictly philosophical plane. What is meant by the term *existentialism?*

Most people who use the word would be rather embarrassed if they had to explain it, since, now that the word is all the rage, even the work of a musician or painter is being called existentialist. A gossip columnist in *Clartés* signs himself *The Existentialist,* so that by this time the word has been so stretched and has taken on so broad a meaning, that it no longer means anything at all. It seems that for want of an advance-guard doctrine analogous to surrealism, the kind of people who are eager. for scandal and flurry turn to this philosophy which in other respects does not at all serve their purposes in this sphere.

Actually, it is the least scandalous, the most austere of doctrines. It is intended strictly for specialists and philosophers. Yet it can be defined easily. What complicates matters is that there are two kinds of existentialist; first, those who are Christian, among whom I would include Jaspers and Gabriel Marcel, both Catholic; and on the other hand the atheistic existentialists, among whom I class Heidegger, and then the French existentialists and myself. What they have in common is that they think that existence precedes essence, or, if you prefer, that subjectivity must be the starting point.

Just what does that mean? Let us consider

some object that is manufactured, for example, a book or a paper-cutter: here is an object which has been made by an artisan whose inspiration came from a concept. He referred to the concept of what a paper-cutter is and likewise to a known method of production, which is part of the concept, something which is, by and large, a routine. Thus, the paper-cutter is at once an object produced in a certain way and, on the other hand, one having a specific use; and one can not postulate a man who produces a paper-cutter but does not know what it is used for. Therefore, let us say that, for the paper-cutter, essence—that is, the ensemble of both the production routines and the properties which enable it to be both produced and defined—precedes existence. Thus, the presence of the paper-cutter or book in front of me is determined. Therefore, we have here a technical view of the world whereby it can be said that production precedes existence.

When we conceive God as the Creator, He is generally thought of as a superior sort of artisan. Whatever doctrine we may be considering, whether one like that of Descartes or that of Leibnitz, we always grant that will more or less follows understanding or, at the very least, accompanies it, and that when God creates He knows exactly what He is creating. Thus, the concept of man in the mind of God is comparable to the concept of paper-cutter in the mind of the manufacturer, and, following certain techniques and a conception, God produces man, just as the artisan, following a definition and a technique, makes a paper-cutter. Thus, the individual man is the realisation of a certain concept in the divine intelligence.

In the eighteenth century, the atheism of the *philosophes* discarded the idea of God, but not so much for the notion that essence precedes existence. To a certain extent, this idea is found everywhere; we find it in Diderot, in Voltaire, and even in Kant. Man has a human nature; this human nature, which is the concept of the human, is found in all men, which means that each man is a particular example of a universal concept, man. In Kant, the result of this universality is that the wild-man, the natural man, as well as the bourgeois, are circumscribed by the same definition and have the same basic qualities. Thus, here too the essence of man precedes the historical existence that we find in nature.

Atheistic existentialism, which I represent, is more coherent. It states that if God does not exist, there is at least one being in whom existence precedes essence, a being who exists before he can be defined by any concept, and that this being is man, or, as Heidegger says, human reality. What is meant here by saying that existence precedes essence? It means that, first of all, man exists, turns up, appears on the scene, and, only afterwards, defines himself. If man, as the existentialist conceives him, is indefinable, it is because at first he is nothing. Only afterward will he be something, and he himself will have made what he will be. Thus, there is no human nature, since there is no God to conceive it. Not only is man what he conceives himself to be, but he is also only what he wills himself to be after this thrust toward existence.

Man is nothing else but what he makes of himself. Such is the first principle of existentialism. It is also what is called subjectivity, the name we are labeled with when charges are brought against us. But what do we mean by this, if not that man has a greater dignity than a stone or table? For we mean that man first exists, that is, that man first of all is the being who hurls himself toward a future and who is conscious of imagining himself as being in the future. Man is at the start a plan which is aware of itself, rather than a patch of moss, a piece of garbage, or a cauliflower; nothing exists prior to this plan; there is nothing in heaven; man will be what he will have planned to be. Not what he will want to be. Because by the word "will" we generally mean a conscious decision, which is subsequent to what we have already made of ourselves. I may want to belong to a political party, write a book, get married; but all that is only a manifestation of an earlier, more spontaneous choice that is called "will." But if existence really does precede essence, man is responsible for what he is. Thus, existentialism's first move is to make every man aware of what he is and to make the full responsibility of his existence rest on him. And when we say that a man is responsible for himself, we do not only mean that he is responsible for his own individuality, but that he is responsible for all men.

The word subjectivism has two meanings, and our opponents play on the two. Subjectivism means, on the one hand, that an individual chooses and makes himself; and, on the other, that it is impossible for man to transcend human subjectivity. The second of these is the essential meaning of existentialism. When we say that man chooses his own self, we mean that every one of us does likewise; but we also mean by that that in making this choice he also chooses all men. In fact, in creating the man that we want to be, there is not a single one of our acts which does not at the same time create an image of man as we think he ought to be. To choose to be this or that is to affirm at the same time the value of what we choose, because we can never choose evil. We always choose the good, and nothing can be good for us without being good for all.

If, on the other hand, existence precedes essence, and if we grant that we exist and fashion our image at one and the same time, the image is valid for everybody and for our whole age. Thus, our responsibility is much greater than we might have supposed, because it involves all mankind. If I am a workingman and choose to join a Christian trade-union rather than be a communist, and if by being a member I want to show that the best thing for man is resignation, that the kingdom of man is not of this world, I am not only involving my own case—I want to be resigned for everyone. As a result, my action has involved all humanity. To take a more individual matter, if I want to marry, to have children; even if this marriage depends solely on my own circumstances or passion or wish, I am involving all humanity in monogamy and not merely myself. Therefore, I am responsible for myself and for everyone else. I am creating a certain image of man of my own choosing. In choosing myself, I choose man.

This helps us understand what the actual content is of such rather grandiloquent words as anguish, forlornness, despair. As you will see, it's all quite simple.

First, what is meant by anguish? The existentialists say at once that man is anguish. What that means is this: the man who involves himself and who realizes that he is not only the person he chooses to be, but also a law-maker who is, at the same time, choosing all mankind as well as himself, can not help escape the feeling of his total and deep responsibility. Of course, there are many people who are not anxious; but we claim that they are hiding their anxiety, that they are fleeing from it. Certainly, many people believe that when they do something, they themselves are the only ones involved, and when someone says to them, "What if everyone acted that way?" they shrug their shoulders and answer, "Everyone doesn't act that way." But really, one should always ask himself, "What would happen if everybody looked at things that way?" There is no escaping this disturbing thought except by a kind of double-dealing. A man who lies and makes excuses for himself by saying "not everybody does that," is someone with an uneasy conscience, because the act of lying implies that a universal value is conferred upon the lie.

Anguish is evident even when it conceals itself. This is the anguish that Kierkegaard called the anguish of Abraham. You know the story: an angel has ordered Abraham to sacrifice his son; if it really were an angel who has come and said, "You are Abraham, you shall sacrifice your son," everything would be all right. But everyone might first wonder, "Is it really an angel, and am I really Abraham? What proof do I have?"

There was a madwoman who had hallucinations; someone used to speak to her on the telephone and give her orders. Her doctor asked her, "Who is it who talks to you?" She answered, "He says it's God." What proof did she really have that it was God? If an angel comes to me, what proof is there that it's an angel? And if I hear voices, what proof is there that they come from heaven and not from hell, or from the subconscious, or a pathological condition? What proves that they are addressed to me? What proof is there that I have been appointed to impose my choice and my conception of man on humanity? I'll never find any proof or sign to convince me of that. If a voice addresses me, it is always for me to decide that this is the angel's voice; if I consider that such an act is a good one, it is I who will choose to say that it is good rather than bad.

Now, I'm not being singled out as an Abraham, and yet at every moment I'm obliged to perform exemplary acts. For every man, everything happens as if all mankind had its eyes fixed on him and were guiding itself by what he does. And every man ought to say to himself, "Am I really the kind of man who has the right to act in such a way that humanity might guide itself by my actions?" And if he does not say that to himself, he is masking his anguish.

There is no question here of the kind of anguish which would lead to quietism, to inaction. It is a matter of a simple sort of anguish that anybody who has had responsibilities is familiar with. For example, when a military officer takes the responsibility for an attack and sends a certain number of men to death, he chooses to do so, and in the main he alone makes the choice. Doubtless, orders come from above, but they are too broad; he interprets them, and on this interpretation depend the lives of ten or fourteen or twenty men. In making a decision he can not help having a certain anguish. All leaders know this anguish. That doesn't keep them from acting; on the contrary, it is the very condition of their action. For it implies that they envisage a number of possibilities, and when they choose one, they realize that it has value only because it is chosen. We shall see that this kind of anguish, which is the kind that existentialism describes, is explained, in addition, by a direct responsibility to the other men whom it involves. It is not a curtain separating us from action, but is part of action itself.

When we speak of forlornness, a term Heidegger was fond of, we mean only that God does not exist and that we have to face all the consequences of this. The existentialist is strongly opposed to a certain kind of secular ethics which would like to abolish God with the least possible expense. About 1880, some French teachers tried to set up a secular ethics which went something like this: God is a useless and costly hypothesis; we are discarding it; but, meanwhile, in order for there to be an ethics, a society, a civilization, it is essential that certain values be taken seriously and that they be considered as having an *a priori* existence. It must be obligatory, *a priori,* to be honest, not to lie, not to beat your wife, to have children, etc., etc. So we're going to try a little device which will make it possible to show that values exist all the same, inscribed in a heaven of ideas, though otherwise God does not exist. In other words—and this, I believe, is the tendency of everything called reformism in France —nothing will be changed if God does not exist. We shall find ourselves with the same norms of honesty, progress, and humanism, and we shall have made of God an outdated hypothesis which will peacefully die off by itself.

The existentialist, on the contrary, thinks it very distressing that God does not exist, because all possibility of finding values in a heaven of ideas disappears along with Him; there can no longer be an *a priori* Good, since there is no infinite and perfect consciousness to think it. Nowhere is it written that the Good exists, that we must be honest, that we must not lie; because the fact is we are on a plane where there are only men. Dostoievsky said, "If God didn't exist, everything would be possible." That is the very starting point of existentialism. Indeed, everything is permissible if God does not exist, and as a result man is forlorn, because neither within him nor without does he find anything to cling to. He can't start making excuses for himself.

If existence really does precede essence, there is no explaining things away by reference to a fixed and given human nature. In other words, there is no determinism, man is free, man is freedom. On the other hand, if God does not exist, we find no values or commands to turn to which legitimize our conduct. So, in the bright realm of values, we have no excuse behind us, nor justification before us. We are alone, with no excuses.

That is the idea I shall try to convey when I say that man is condemned to be free. Condemned, because he did not create himself, yet, in other respects is free; because, once thrown into the world, he is responsible for everything he does. The existentialist does not believe in the power of passion. He will never

agree that a sweeping passion is a ravaging tor-
rent which fatally leads a man to certain acts
and is therefore an excuse. He thinks that man
is responsible for his passion.

The existentialist does not think that man is
going to help himself by finding in the world
some omen by which to orient himself. Because
he thinks that man will interpret the omen to
suit himself. Therefore, he thinks that man,
with no support and no aid, is condemned every
moment to invent man. Ponge, in a very fine
article, has said, "Man is the future of man."
That's exactly it. But if it is taken to mean that
this future is recorded in heaven, that God sees
it, then it is false, because it would really no
longer be a future. If it is taken to mean that,
whatever a man may be, there is a future to be
forged, a virgin future before him, then this
remark is sound. But then we are forlorn.

To give you an example which will enable
you to understand forlornness better, I shall
cite the case of one of my students who came
to see me under the following circumstances:
his father was on bad terms with his mother,
and, moreover, was inclined to be a collabora-

tionist; his older brother had been killed in the German offensive of 1940, and the young man, with somewhat immature but generous feelings, wanted to avenge him. His mother lived alone with him, very much upset by the half-treason of her husband and the death of her older son; the boy was her only consolation.

The boy was faced with the choice of leaving for England and joining the Free French Forces —that is, leaving his mother behind—or remaining with his mother and helping her to carry on. He was fully aware that the woman lived only for him and that his going-off—and perhaps his death—would plunge her into despair. He was also aware that every act that he did for his mother's sake was a sure thing, in the sense that it was helping her to carry on, whereas every effort he made toward going off and fighting was an uncertain move which might run aground and prove completely useless; for example, on his way to England he might, while passing through Spain, be detained indefinitely in a Spanish camp; he might reach England or Algiers and be stuck in an office at a desk job. As a result, he was faced with two very different kinds of action: one, concrete, immediate, but concerning only one individual; the other concerned an incomparably vaster group, a national collectivity, but for that very reason was dubious, and might be interrupted en route. And, at the same time, he was wavering between two kinds of ethics. On the one hand, an ethics of sympathy, of personal devotion; on the other, a broader ethics, but one whose efficacy was more dubious. He had to choose between the two.

Who could help him choose? Christian doctrine? No. Christian doctrine says, "Be charitable, love your neighbor, take the more rugged path, etc., etc." But which is the more rugged path? Whom should he love as a brother? The fighting man or his mother? Which does the greater good, the vague act of fighting in a group, or the concrete one of helping a particular human being to go on living? Who can decide *a priori?* Nobody. No book of ethics can tell him. The Kantian ethics says, "Never treat any person as a means, but as an end." Very well, if I stay with my mother, I'll treat her as an end and not as a means; but by virtue of this very fact, I'm running the risk of treating the people around me who are fighting, as means; and, conversely, if I go to join those who are fighting, I'll be treating them as an end, and, by doing that, I run the risk of treating my mother as a means.

If values are vague, and if they are always too broad for the concrete and specific case that we are considering, the only thing left for us is to trust our instincts. That's what this young man tried to do; and when I saw him, he said, "In the end, feeling is what counts. I ought to choose whichever pushes me in one direction. If I feel that I love my mother enough to sacrifice everything else for her—my desire for vengeance, for action, for adventure—then I'll stay with her. If, on the contrary, I feel that my love for my mother isn't enough, I'll leave."

But how is the value of a feeling determined? What gives his feeling for his mother value? Precisely the fact that he remained with her. I may say that I like so-and-so well enough to sacrifice a certain amount of money for him, but I may say so only if I've done it. I may say "I love my mother well enough to remain with her" if I have remained with her. The only way to determine the value of this affection is, precisely, to perform an act which confirms and defines it. But, since I require this affection to justify my act, I find myself caught in a vicious circle.

On the other hand, Gide has well said that a mock feeling and a true feeling are almost indistinguishable; to decide that I love my mother and will remain with her, or to remain with her by putting on an act, amount somewhat to the same thing. In other words, the feeling is formed by the acts one performs; so, I can not refer to it in order to act upon it. Which means that I can neither seek within myself the true condition which will impel me to act, nor apply to a system of ethics for concepts which will permit me to act. You will say, "At least, he did go to a teacher for advice." But if you seek advice from a priest, for example, you have chosen this priest; you already knew, more or less, just about what advice he was going to give you. In other words, choosing your adviser is involving yourself. The proof of this is that if you are a Christian, you will say, "Consult a priest."

But some priests are collaborating, some are just marking time, some are resisting. Which to choose? If the young man chooses a priest who is resisting or collaborating, he has already decided on the kind of advice he's going to get. Therefore, in coming to see me he knew the answer I was going to give him, and I had only one answer to give: "You're free, choose, that is, invent." No general ethics can show you what is to be done; there are no omens in the world. The Catholics will reply, "But there are." Granted—but, in any case, I myself choose the meaning they have.

When I was a prisoner, I knew a rather remarkable young man who was a Jesuit. He had entered the Jesuit order in the following way: he had had a number of very bad breaks; in childhood, his father died, leaving him in poverty, and he was a scholarship student at a religious institution where he was constantly made to feel that he was being kept out of charity; then, he failed to get any of the honors and distinctions that children like; later on, at about eighteen, he bungled a love affair; finally, at twenty-two, he failed in military training, a childish enough matter, but it was the last straw.

This young fellow might well have felt that he had botched everything. It was a sign of something, but of what? He might have taken refuge in bitterness or despair. But he very wisely looked upon all this as a sign that he was not made for secular triumphs, and that only the triumphs of religion, holiness, and faith were open to him. He saw the hand of God in all this, and so he entered the order. Who can help seeing that he alone decided what the sign meant?

Some other interpretation might have been drawn from this series of setbacks; for example, that he might have done better to turn carpenter or revolutionist. Therefore, he is fully responsible for the interpretation. Forlornness implies that we ourselves choose our being. Forlornness and anguish go together.

As for despair, the term has a very simple meaning. It means that we shall confine ourselves to reckoning only with what depends upon our will, or on the ensemble of probabilities which make our action possible. When we want something, we always have to reckon with probabilities. I may be counting on the arrival of a friend. The friend is coming by rail or street-car; this supposes that the train will arrive on schedule, or that the street-car will not jump the track. I am left in the realm of possibility; but possibilities are to be reckoned with only to the point where my action comports with the ensemble of these possibilities, and no further. The moment the possibilities I am considering are not rigorously involved by my action, I ought to disengage myself from them, because no God, no scheme, can adapt the world and its possibilities to my will. When Descartes said, "Conquer yourself rather than the world," he meant essentially the same thing.

The Marxists to whom I have spoken reply, "You can rely on the support of others in your action, which obviously has certain limits because you're not going to live forever. That means: rely on both what others are doing elsewhere to help you, in China, in Russia, and what they will do later on, after your death, to carry on the action and lead it to its fulfillment, which will be the revolution. You even *have* to

rely upon that, otherwise you're immoral." I
reply at once that I will always rely on fellow-
fighters insofar as these comrades are involved
with me in a common struggle, in the unity of
a party or a group in which I can more or less
make my weight felt; that is, one whose ranks I
am in as a fighter and whose movements I am
aware of at every moment. In such a situation,
relying on the unity and will of the party is
exactly like counting on the fact that the train
will arrive on time or that the car won't jump the
track. But, given that man is free and that there
is no human nature for me to depend on, I can
not count on men whom I do not know by
relying on human goodness or man's concern
for the good of society. I don't know what will
become of the Russian revolution; I may make
an example of it to the extent that at the present
time it is apparent that the proletariat plays a
part in Russia that it plays in no other nation.
But I can't swear that this will inevitably lead
to a triumph of the proletariat. I've got to limit
myself to what I see.

Given that men are free and that tomorrow
they will freely decide what man will be, I

can not be sure that, after my death, fellow-fighters will carry on my work to bring it to its maximum perfection. Tomorrow, after my death, some men may decide to set up Fascism, and the others may be cowardly and muddled enough to let them do it. Fascism will then be the human reality, so much the worse for us.

Actually, things will be as man will have decided they are to be. Does that mean that I should abandon myself to quietism? No. First, I should involve myself; then, act on the old saw, "Nothing ventured, nothing gained." Nor does it mean that I shouldn't belong to a party, but rather that I shall have no illusions and shall do what I can. For example, suppose I ask myself, "Will socialization, as such, ever come about?" I know nothing about it. All I know is that I'm going to do everything in my power to bring it about. Beyond that, I can't count on anything. Quietism is the attitude of people who say, "Let others do what I can't do." The doctrine I am presenting is the very opposite of quietism, since it declares, "There is no reality except in action." Moreover, it goes further, since it adds, "Man is nothing else than his plan; he exists only to the extent that he fulfills himself; he is therefore nothing else than the ensemble of his acts, nothing else than his life."

According to this, we can understand why our doctrine horrifies certain people. Because often the only way they can bear their wretchedness is to think, "Circumstances have been against me. What I've been and done doesn't show my true worth. To be sure, I've had no great love, no great friendship, but that's because I haven't met a man or woman who was worthy. The books I've written haven't been very good because I haven't had the proper leisure. I haven't had children to devote myself to because I didn't find a man with whom I could have spent my life. So there remains within me, unused and quite viable, a host of propensities, inclinations, possibilities, that one wouldn't guess from, the mere series of things I've done."

Now, for the existentialist there is really no love other than one which manifests itself in a person's being in love. There is no genius other than one which is expressed in works of art; the genius of Proust is the sum of Proust's works; the genius of Racine is his series of tragedies. Outside of that, there is nothing. Why say that Racine could have written another tragedy, when he didn't write it? A man is involved in life, leaves his impress on it, and outside of that there is nothing. To be sure, this may seem a harsh thought to someone whose life hasn't been a success. But, on the other hand, it prompts people to understand that reality alone is what counts, that dreams, expectations, and hopes warrant no more than to define a man as a disappointed dream, as miscarried hopes, as vain expectations. In other words, to define him negatively and not positively. However, when we say, "You are nothing else than your life," that does not imply that the artist will be judged solely on the basis of his works of art; a thousand other things will contribute toward summing him up. What we mean is that a man is nothing else than a series of undertakings, that he is the sum, the organization, the ensemble of the relationships which make up these undertakings.

When all is said and done, what we are accused of, at bottom, is not our pessimism, but an optimistic toughness. If people throw up to us our works of fiction in which we write about people who are soft, weak, cowardly, and sometimes even downright bad, it's not because these people are soft, weak, cowardly, or bad; because if we were to say, as Zola did, that they are that way because of heredity, the workings of environment, society, because of biological or psychological determinism, people would be reassured. They would say, "Well, that's what we're like, no one can do anything about it." But when the existentialist writes about a coward, he says that this coward is responsible for his cowardice. He's not like that because he has a cowardly heart or lung or brain; he's not like that on account of his physiological make-up; but he's like that because he has made himself a coward by his acts. There's no such thing as a cowardly constitution; there are nervous constitutions; there is poor blood, as the common people say, or strong constitutions. But the man whose blood is poor is not a coward on that account, for what makes cowardice is the act of renouncing or yielding. A constitution is not an act; the coward is defined on the basis of the acts he performs. People feel, in a vague sort of way, that this coward we're talking about is guilty of being a coward, and the thought frightens them. What people would like is that a coward or a hero be born that way.

One of the complaints most frequently made about *The Ways of Freedom* * can be summed up as follows: "After all, these people are so spineless, how are you going to make heroes out of them?" This objection almost makes me laugh, for it assumes that people are born heroes. That's what people really want to think. If you're born cowardly, you may set your mind perfectly at rest; there's nothing you can do about it; you'll be cowardly all your life, whatever you may do. If you're born a hero, you may set your mind just as much at rest; you'll be a hero all your life; you'll drink like a hero and eat like a hero. What the existentialist says is that the coward makes himself cowardly, that the hero makes himself heroic. There's always

* *Les Chemins de la Liberté*, M. Sartre's projected trilogy of novels, two of which, *L'Age de Raison* (*The Age of Reason*) and *Le Sursis* (*The Reprieve*) have already appeared.—Translator's note.

a possibility for the coward not to be cowardly any more and for the hero to stop being heroic. What counts is total involvement; some one particular action or set of circumstances is not total involvement.

Thus, I think we have answered a number of the charges concerning existentialism. You see that it can not be taken for a philosophy of quietism, since it defines man in terms of action; nor for a pessimistic description of man— there is no doctrine more optimistic, since man's destiny is within himself; nor for an attempt to discourage man from acting, since it tells him that the only hope is in his acting and that action is the only thing that enables a man to live. Consequently, we are dealing here with an ethics of action and involvement.

Nevertheless, on the basis of a few notions like these, we are still charged with immuring man in his private subjectivity. There again we're very much misunderstood. Subjectivity of the individual is indeed our point of departure, and this for strictly philosophic reasons. Not because we are bourgeois, but because we want a doctrine based on truth and not a lot of fine theories, full of hope but with no real basis. There can be no other truth to take off from than this: *I think; therefore, I exist.* There we have the absolute truth of consciousness becoming aware of itself. Every theory which takes man out of the moment in which he becomes aware of himself is, at its very beginning, a theory which confounds truth, for outside the Cartesian *cogito*, all views are only probable, and a doctrine of probability which is not bound to a truth dissolves into thin air. In order to describe the probable, you must have a firm hold on the true. Therefore, before there can be any truth whatsoever, there must be an absolute truth; and this one is simple and easily arrived at; it's on everyone's doorstep; it's a matter of grasping it directly.

Secondly, this theory is the only one which gives man dignity, the only one which does not reduce him to an object. The effect of all materialism is to treat all men, including the one philosophizing, as objects, that is, as an ensemble of determined reactions in no way distinguished from the ensemble of qualities and phenomena which constitute a table or a chair or a stone. We definitely wish to establish the human realm as an ensemble of values distinct from the material realm. But the subjectivity that we have thus arrived at, and which we have claimed to be truth, is not a strictly individual subjectivity, for we have demonstrated that one discovers in the *cogito* not only himself, but others as well.

The philosophies of Descartes and Kant to the contrary, through the *I think* we reach our own self in the presence of others, and the others are just as real to us as our own self. Thus, the man who becomes aware of himself through the *cogito* also perceives all others, and he perceives them as the condition of his own existence. He realizes that he can not be anything (in the sense that we say that someone is witty or nasty or jealous) unless others recognize it as such. In order to get any truth about myself, I must have contact with another person. The other is indispensable to my own existence, as well as to my knowledge about myself. This being so, in discovering my inner being I discover the other person at the same time, like a freedom placed in front of me which thinks and wills only for or against me. Hence, let us at once announce the discovery of a world which we shall call inter-subjectivity; this is the world in which man decides what he is and what others are.

Besides, if it is impossible to find in every man some universal essence which would be human nature, yet there does exist a universal human condition. It's not by chance that to-day's thinkers speak more readily of man's condition than of his nature. By condition they mean, more or less definitely, the *a priori* limits which outline man's fundamental situation in the universe. Historical situations vary; a man may be born a slave in a pagan society or a feudal lord or a proletarian. What does not vary is the necessity for him to exist in the world, to be at work there, to be there in the midst of other people, and to be mortal there. The limits are neither subjective or objective, or, rather, they have an objective and a subjective side. Objective because they are to be found everywhere and are recognizable everywhere; subjective because they are *lived* and are nothing if man does not live them, that is, freely determine his existence with reference to them. And though the configurations may differ, at least none of them are completely strange to me, because they all appear as attempts either to pass beyond these limits or recede from them or deny them or adapt to them. Consequently, every configuration, however individual it may be, has a universal value.

Every configuration, even the Chinese, the Indian, or the Negro, can be understood by a Westerner. "Can be understood" means that by virtue of a situation that he can imagine, a European of 1945 can, in like manner, push himself to his limits and reconstitute within himself the configuration of the Chinese, the Indian, or the African. Every configuration has universality in the sense that every configuration can be understood by every man. This does not at all mean that this configuration defines man forever, but that it can be met with again. There is always a way to understand the idiot, the child, the savage, the foreigner, provided one has the necessary information.

In this sense we may say that there is a universality of man; but it is not given, it is perpetually being made. I build the universal in choosing myself; I build it in understanding the configuration of every other man, whatever age he might have lived in. This absoluteness of choice does not do away with the relativeness of each epoch. At heart, what existentialism shows is the connection between the absolute character of free involvement, by virtue of which every man realizes himself in realizing a type of mankind, an involvement always comprehensible in any age whatsoever and by any person whosoever, and the relativeness of the cultural ensemble which may result from such a choice; it must be stressed that the relativity of Cartesianism and the absolute character of Cartesian involvement go together. In this sense, you may, if you like, say that each of us performs an absolute act in breathing, eating, sleeping, or behaving in any way whatever. There is no difference between being free, like a configuration, like an existence which chooses its essence, and being absolute. There is no difference between being an absolute temporarily localised, that is, localised in history, and being universally comprehensible.

This does not entirely settle the objection to subjectivism. In fact, the objection still takes several forms. First, there is the following: we are told, "So you're able to do anything, no matter what!" This is expressed in various ways. First we are accused of anarchy; then they say, "You're unable to pass judgment on others, because there's no reason to prefer one configuration to another"; finally they tell us, "Everything is arbitrary in this choosing of yours. You take something from one pocket and pretend you're putting it into the other."

These three objections aren't very serious. Take the first objection. "You're able to do anything, no matter what" is not to the point. In one sense choice is possible, but what is not possible is not to choose. I can always choose, but I ought to know that if I do not choose, I am still choosing. Though this may seem purely formal, it is highly important for keeping fantasy and caprice within bounds. If it is true that in facing a situation, for example, one in which, as a person capable of having sexual relations, of having children, I am obliged to choose an attitude, and if I in any way assume responsibility for a choice which, in involving myself, also involves all mankind, this has nothing to do with caprice, even if no *a priori* value determines my choice.

If anybody thinks that he recognizes here Gide's theory of the arbitrary act, he fails to see the enormous difference between this doctrine and Gide's. Gide does not know what a situation is. He acts out of pure caprice. For us, on the contrary, man is in an organized situation in which he himself is involved. Through his choice, he involves all mankind, and he can not avoid making a choice: either he will remain chaste, or he will marry without having children, or he will marry and have children; anyhow, whatever he may do, it is impossible for him not to take full responsibility for the way he handles this problem. Doubtless, he chooses without refering to pre-established values, but it is unfair to accuse him of caprice. Instead, let us say that moral choice is to be compared to the making of a work of art. And before going any further, let it be said at once that we are not dealing here with an aesthetic ethics, because our opponents are so dishonest that they even accuse us of that. The example I've chosen is a comparison only.

Having said that, may I ask whether anyone has ever accused an artist who has painted a picture of not having drawn his inspiration from rules set up *a priori*? Has anyone ever asked, "What painting ought he to make?" It is clearly understood that there is no definite painting to be made, that the artist is engaged in the making of his painting, and that the painting to be made is precisely the painting he will have made. It is clearly understood that there are no *a priori* aesthetic values, but that there are values which appear subsequently in the coherence of the painting, in the correspondence between what the artist intended and the result. Nobody can tell what the painting of tomorrow will be like. Painting can be judged only after it has once been made. What connection does that have with ethics? We are in the same creative situation. We never say that a work of art is arbitrary. When we speak of a canvas of Picasso, we never say that it is arbitrary; we understand quite well that he was making himself what he is at the very time he was painting, that the ensemble of his work is embodied in his life.

The same holds on the ethical plane. What art and ethics have in common is that we have creation and invention in both cases. We can not decide *a priori* what there is to be done. I think that I pointed that out quite sufficiently when I mentioned the case of the student who came to see me, and who might have applied to all the ethical systems, Kantian or otherwise, without getting any sort of guidance. He was obliged to devise his law himself. Never let it be said by us that this man—who, taking affection, individual action, and kind-heartedness toward a specific person as his ethical first principle, chooses to remain with his mother, or who, preferring to make a sacrifice, chooses to go to England—has made an arbitrary choice. Man makes himself. He isn't ready made at the start. In choosing his ethics, he makes himself, and force of circumstances is such that he can not abstain from choosing one. We define man only in relationship to involvement. It is therefore absurd to charge us with arbitrariness of choice.

In the second place, it is said that we are unable to pass judgment on others. In a way this is true, and in another way, false. It is true in this sense, that, whenever a man sanely and sincerely involves himself and chooses his configuration, it is impossible for him to prefer another configuration, regardless of what his own may be in other respects. It is true in this sense, that we do not believe in progress. Progress is betterment. Man is always the same. The situation confronting him varies. Choice always remains a choice in a situation. The problem has not changed since the time one could choose between those for and those against slavery, for example, at the time of the Civil War, and the present time, when one can side with the Maquis Resistance Party, or with the Communists.

But, nevertheless, one can still pass judgment, for, as I have said, one makes a choice in relationship to others. First, one can judge (and this is perhaps not a judgment of value, but a logical judgment) that certain choices are based on error and others on truth. If we have defined man's situation as a free choice, with no excuses and no recourse, every man who takes refuge behind the excuse of his passions, every man who sets up a determinism, is a dishonest man.

The objection may be raised, "But why mayn't he choose himself dishonestly?" I reply that I am not obliged to pass moral judgment on him, but that I do define his dishonesty as an error. One can not help considering the truth of the matter. Dishonesty is obviously a false-hood because it belies the complete freedom of involvement. On the same grounds, I main-tain that there is also dishonesty if I choose to state that certain values exist prior to me; it is self-contradictory for me to want them and at the same state that they are imposed on me. Suppose someone says to me, "What if I want to be dishonest?" I'll answer, "There's no rea-son for you not to be, but I'm saying that that's what you are, and that the strictly coherent at-titude is that of honesty."

Besides, I can bring moral judgment to bear. When I declare that freedom in every concrete circumstance can have no other aim than to want itself, if man has once become aware that in his forlornness he imposes values, he can no longer want but one thing, and that is freedom, as the basis of all values. That doesn't mean that he wants it in the abstract. It means simply that the ultimate meaning of the acts of honest men is the quest for freedom as such. A man who belongs to a communist or revolutionary union wants concrete goals; these goals imply an abstract desire for freedom; but this freedom is wanted in something concrete. We want freedom for freedom's sake and in every particular circumstance. And in wanting freedom we discover that it depends entirely on the freedom of others, and that the freedom of others depends on ours. Of course, freedom as the definition of man does not depend on others, but as soon as there is involvement, I am obliged to want others to have freedom at the same time that I want my own freedom. I can take freedom as my goal only if I take that of others as a goal as well. Consequently, when, in all honesty, I've recognized that man is a being in whom existence precedes essence, that he is a free being who, in various circumstances, can want only his freedom, I have at the same time recognized that I can want only the freedom of others.

Therefore, in the name of this will for freedom, which freedom itself implies, I may pass judgment on those who seek to hide from themselves the complete arbitrariness and the complete freedom of their existence. Those who hide their complete freedom from themselves out of a spirit of seriousness or by means of deterministic excuses, I shall call cowards; those who try to show that their existence was necessary, when it is the very contingency of man's appearance on earth, I shall call stinkers. But cowards or stinkers can be judged only from a strictly unbiased point of view.

Therefore though the content of ethics is variable, a certain form of it is universal. Kant says that freedom desires both itself and the freedom of others. Granted. But he believes that the formal and the universal are enough to constitute an ethics. We, on the other hand, think that principles which are too abstract run aground in trying to decide action. Once again, take the case of the student. In the name of what, in the name of what great moral maxim do you think he could have decided, in perfect peace of mind, to abandon his mother or to stay with her? There is no way of judging. The content is always concrete and thereby unforeseeable; there is always the element of invention. The one thing that counts is knowing whether the inventing that has been done, has been done in the name of freedom.

For example, let us look at the following two cases. You will see to what extent they correspond, yet differ. Take *The Mill on the Floss.* We find a certain young girl, Maggie Tulliver, who is an embodiment of the value of passion and who is aware of it. She is in love with a young man, Stephen, who is engaged to an insignificant young girl. This Maggie Tulliver, instead of heedlessly preferring her own happiness, chooses, in the name of human solidarity, to sacrifice herself and give up the man she loves. On the other hand, Sanseverina, in *The Charterhouse of Parma,* believing that passion is man's true value, would say that a great love deserves sacrifices; that it is to be preferred to the banality of the conjugal love that would tie Stephen to the young ninny he had to marry.

She would choose to sacrifice the girl and fulfill her happiness; and, as Stendhal shows, she is even ready to sacrifice herself for the sake of passion, if this life demands it. Here we are in the presence of two strictly opposed moralities. I claim that they are much the same thing; in both cases what has been set up as the goal is freedom.

You can imagine two highly similar attitudes: one girl prefers to renounce her love out of resignation; another prefers to disregard the prior attachment of the man she loves out of sexual desire. On the surface these two actions resemble those we've just described. However, they are completely different. Sanseverina's attitude is much nearer that of Maggie Tulliver, one of heedless rapacity.

Thus, you see that the second charge is true and, at the same time, false. One may choose anything if it is on the grounds of free involvement.

The third objection is the following: "You take something from one pocket and put it into the other. That is, fundamentally, values aren't serious, since you choose them." My answer to this is that I'm quite vexed that that's the way it is; but if I've discarded God the Father, there has to be someone to invent values. You've got to take things as they are. Moreover, to say that we invent values means nothing else but this: life has no meaning *a priori*. Before you come alive, life is nothing; it's up to you to give it a meaning, and value is nothing else but the meaning that you choose. In that way, you see, there is a possibility of creating a human community.

I've been reproached for asking whether existentialism is humanistic. It's been said, "But you said in *Nausea* that the humanists were all wrong. You made fun of a certain kind of humanist. Why come back to it now?" Actually, the word humanism has two very different meanings. By humanism one can mean a theory which takes man as an end and as a higher value. Humanism in this sense can be found in Cocteau's tale *Around the World in Eighty Hours* when a character, because he is flying over some mountains in an airplane, declares, "Man is simply amazing." That means that I, who did not build the airplanes, shall personally benefit from these particular inventions, and that I, as man, shall personally consider myself responsible for, and honored by, acts of a few particular men. This would imply that we ascribe a value to man on the basis of the highest deeds of certain men. This humanism is absurd, because only the dog or the horse would be able to make such an over-all judgment about man, which they are careful not to do, at least to my knowledge.

But it can not be granted that a man may make a judgment about man. Existentialism spares him from any such judgment. The existentialist will never consider man as an end because he is always in the making. Nor should we believe that there is a mankind to which we might set up a cult in the manner of Auguste Comte. The cult of mankind ends in the self-enclosed humanism of Comte, and, let it be said, of fascism. This kind of humanism we can do without.

But there is another meaning of humanism. Fundamentally it is this: man is constantly outside of himself; in projecting himself, in losing himself outside of himself, he makes for man's existing; and, on the other hand, it is by pursuing transcendent goals that he is able to exist; man, being this state of passing-beyond, and seizing upon things only as they bear upon this passing-beyond, is at the heart, at the center of this passing-beyond. There is no universe other than a human universe, the universe of human subjectivity. This connection between transcendency, as a constituent element of man—not in the sense that God is transcendent, but in the sense of passing beyond—and subjectivity, in the sense that man is not closed in on himself but is always present in a human universe, is what we call existentialist humanism. Humanism, because we remind man that there is no law-maker other than himself, and that in his forlornness he will decide by himself; because we point out that man will fulfill himself as man, not in turning toward himself, but in seeking outside of himself a goal which is just this liberation, just this particular fulfillment.

From these few reflections it is evident that nothing is more unjust than the objections that have been raised against us. Existentialism is nothing else than an attempt to draw all the consequences of a coherent atheistic position. It isn't trying to plunge man into despair at all. But if one calls every attitude of unbelief despair, like the Christians, then the word is not being used in its original sense. Existentialism isn't so atheistic that it wears itself out showing that God doesn't exist. Rather, it declares that even if God did exist, that would change nothing. There you've got our point of view. Not that we believe that God exists, but we think that the problem of His existence is not the issue. In this sense existentialism is optimistic, a doctrine of action, and it is plain dishonesty for Christians to make no distinction between their own despair and ours and then to call us despairing.

DISCUSSION

QUESTION:

I don't know whether wanting to make yourself understood will cause you to be better understood or will further misunderstanding,
but I do believe that the clarification which
appeared in *Action* gives rise to even more misunderstanding. The words despair and forlornness have a much stronger ring in an existentialist text. It seems to me that, for you, despair
or anguish is something more fundamental than
simply the decision of the man who feels himself alone and who must decide. It's a struggle
of consciousness that doesn't occur every day.
Agreed that one is choosing himself all the time,
but anguish and despair don't occur in an off-
hand way.

M. SARTRE:

I obviously don't mean that when I choose
between a cream-puff and a chocolate eclair
I'm choosing in anguish. Anguish is constant in
the sense that my original choice is a constant
thing. In fact, anguish, as I see it, is the con-

currence of the complete absence of justification and responsibility toward others.

QUESTION:

I was speaking of the point of view of the clarification which appeared in *Action*. It seems to me that your point of view was rather weakened there.

M. SARTRE:

To tell the truth, it's possible that my ideas were somewhat weakened in *Action*. It often happens that people who aren't qualified to do so come to interview me. I find myself at such times with two possible solutions: either to refuse to answer or to agree to carry on discussion on a popular level. I've chosen the second because, after all, when one presents theories in a philosophy class, he's prepared to weaken a thought in order to make it understood, and that's not too bad a thing. If one has a theory of involvement, he has to involve himself to the limit. If existentialist philosophy really is, before all else, a philosophy which says that existence precedes essence, it ought to be lived

in order to be truly sincere. To live as an existentialist is to accept the fact that you have
to pay for this doctrine, and not just lay it away
in books. If you want this philosophy to be
really involved in action, you have to give an
account of it to the people who discuss it on
the political or moral level.

You charge me with using the word humanism. That's because the problem presents itself
in this way: you either have to work with the
doctrine on a strictly philosophic level and
count on chance for it to operate actively or,
since people ask something else of it, and it
seeks to be a mode of involvement, you have
to agree to popularize it, on condition that popularization doesn't deform it.

QUESTION:
Those who want to understand you will understand you, and those who don't want to
understand you won't.

M. SARTRE:
The way you seem to conceive philosophy's
role in the world is behind the times. Not so

long ago philosophers were attacked only by other philosophers. The common people didn't know what it was all about and were unconcerned with it. Nowadays, philosophy is brought down to the marketplace. Marx himself never stopped popularizing his ideas; the *Manifesto* is the popularization of an idea.

QUESTION:

Marx's original choice was a revolutionary choice.

M. SARTRE:

A man who can tell whether he chose himself as a revolutionist first and then as a philosopher, or as a philosopher first and then as a revolutionist, must be pretty smart. He's philosopher and revolutionist both. They go together. "He chose himself as revolutionist first." What does that mean?

QUESTION:

The *Communist Manifesto* doesn't seem to me like a popularization, but rather a weapon. I can not believe that it wasn't an act of involvement.

Once Marx the philosopher came to the conclusion that revolution was necessary, his first act was his *Communist Manifesto* which was a political act. The *Communist Manifesto* is the link between Marx's philosophy and communism. Whatever the ethics you may have, one doesn't feel as strict a logical connection between this ethics and your philosophy as between the *Communist Manifesto* and Marx's philosophy.

M. SARTRE:

It's a question of an ethics of freedom. If there's no contradiction between this ethics and our philosophy, nothing more is required. The kind of involvement differs with the age. In an age when involving one's self meant bringing about a revolution, the *Manifesto* had to be written. In an age like ours, when there are different parties each claiming to be the party of revolution, involvement does not mean joining one of them, but rather trying to clarify concepts in order both to show precisely what the state of affairs is and at the same time to act on the different revolutionary parties.

EXISTENTIALISM

M. NAVILLE:

The question that one might well ask himself on the basis of the viewpoints that you've
just made clear is whether your doctrine won't
appear, in the years ahead, like a resurrection
of old-fashioned reformism. This may appear
odd, but at the present time that's the way the
question must be put. Besides you're taking all
sorts of viewpoints. But if one attempts to find
a point where these viewpoints, these aspects
of existentialism, converge at the present time,
it's my impression that he'll find it in a kind of
resurrection of liberalism.

Your philosophy is attempting to revive the
essential nature of reformism, of humanistic
liberalism, in a highly specific situation, namely,
the present historical situation. The thing that
gives it its peculiar character is that the world-
wide social crisis no longer permits of old-time
liberalism; it demands a liberalism that is in
torture, in agony. I believe that a number of
rather weighty reasons can be found in support
of this view, even if one keeps to your own
terms.

From the account just given, existentialism

appears in the guise of a humanistic doctrine
and a philosophy of freedom, which is at bottom a free engagement, a plan with nothing
definite about it. Like many others, you bring
to the fore human dignity, the lofty dignity of
the person, themes which, all things considered, aren't so far from the old liberal themes.
To justify them you make distinctions between
the two meanings of humanism, between two
meanings of the "human condition," between
two meanings of a number of rather outmoded
terms which have, moreover, quite a significant
history, and whose equivocal character is not
the fruit of chance. In order to save them, you
invent a new meaning for them. I'm leaving
aside all the special questions which have reference to philosophical method, though they're
interesting and important, and in order to keep
to the terms I've heard, I'll take up one fundamental point which will show that, at bottom,
despite your distinction between the two meanings of humanism, you're holding to the older
of the two.

Man appears as a choice to be made. Very
well. He is, before everything else, his existence

at the present moment and he is outside of natural determinism. Definition of him is not previous to him but is a function of his individual present existence. There is not a human nature superior to him; rather, he is given a specific existence at a given moment.

I wonder whether existence in this sense isn't another form of the concept of human nature dressed up, for historical reasons, in a new style; whether it isn't very similar, and more than it seems at first, to human nature as it was defined in the eighteenth century, which concept you say you reject; because, to a great extent, it's again met with behind the expression "human condition" as existentialism uses it. Your conception of the human condition is a substitute for human nature, just as you substitute lived experience for every-day experience or scientific experience.

If one considers human conditions as conditions which are definable by something we may call X, the X of the subject, but not by their natural context, their positive determination, we are dealing with another form of human nature; it is, if you will, a nature-condition, that is, it is not definable simply as an abstract type of nature, but reveals itself by something much more difficult to formulate for reasons which, to my way of thinking, are historical.

Today, human nature is explained within social frameworks which are those of a general breaking-up of social orders, of classes, of the conflicts which cut across them, of a stirring of races and nations; with the result that the very idea of a uniform and schematic human nature can no longer be presented with the same character of generality, can no longer assume the same type of universality, as in the eighteenth century, the age in which the expression of such an idea seemed to be based on a continuous progress. Today we are dealing with an expression of human nature that people who think or speak naively about this question express as the human condition. They express the idea in a vague and chaotic way, and, most often, with what I might call a dramatic air that circumstances force them to assume; and to the extent that one is unwilling to pass from the general expression of this condition to the deterministic examination of what the conditions actually are, they preserve the type, the scheme, of an abstract expression analogous to that of human nature.

Thus, existentialism holds fast to the idea of a human nature, but this time it's not a nature that's proud of itself, but rather a fearful, uncertain, forlorn condition. And, actually, when the existentialist speaks of the human condition, he's speaking of a condition which is not yet really involved in what the existentialist calls projects, and which, consequently, is a pre-condition. It's a question of pre-involvement, and not of involvement or of a genuine condition. In that case, it's no longer by accident that the character of this condition is defined, above all, by its general humanism. Furthermore, when they spoke in the past of human nature, they were after something more limited than what one means when he speaks of a condition in general, because nature is quite a different thing. To a certain extent, it is more than a condition.

Human nature is not a modality in the sense that the human condition is a modality. That's why, to my way of thinking, it's better to talk of naturalism than humanism. There's a more general implication of realities in naturalism than in humanism, at least in the meaning that the term humanism has for you; we are dealing with a reality.

Furthermore, this discussion about human nature should be widened. Because the historical point of view should also be brought in. The first reality is natural reality, of which human reality is only a function. But, for that, the truth of history must be recognized, and the existentialist, in a vague sort of way, doesn't admit the truth of history, of natural history in general any more than of human history; and yet, it is history which makes individuals. It's their own history, from the moment they are conceived, which makes them be born and appear, not in a world which sets up an abstract condition for them, but in a world of which they themselves are always part, by which they are conditioned and which they condition, the way a mother conditions and is conditioned by her child from the time of gestation.

From this point of view only do we have

the right to speak of the human condition as a
prime reality. Natural condition should rather
be spoken of as the prime reality and not human condition. I'm only repeating everyday,
commonplace opinions, but they don't seem at
all refuted by the existentialist version of things.
In short, if it is true that there is no abstract
human nature, an essence independent of, or
prior to, man's existence, it is also certain that
there is no general human condition, even if by
condition you mean certain concrete circumstances or situations, because, in your eyes,
they are not articulated. At any rate, Marxism
has a different idea on this subject, that of nature in man and man in nature, man not neces-
sarily being explained from an individual point
of view.

That means that there are laws of operation
for men as for every other object of science,
laws which, in the fullest sense of the word,
constitute his nature, a varied nature, to be
sure, and very slightly resembling a phenomenology, that is, a proved, empirical, lived perception, such as common sense or, rather, the
supposed common sense of the philosophers

gives us. In this sense, the conception of human nature that the men of the eighteenth century set up was doubtless much nearer that of Marx than its existentialist substitute, the human condition, a pure phenomenology of situation.

Today, humanism is unfortunately a term which serves to designate philosophic currents not only in two senses, but in three, four, five, six. At the moment, everybody's a humanist. Even certain Marxists, who blossom forth as classical rationalists, are humanists in a wishy-washy sort of way, in a sense of the term derived from the liberal ideas of the last century, that of a liberalism refracted through the whole present crisis. If Marxists may claim to be humanists, the different religions, the Christians, the Hindus, and a lot of others are also claiming to be, above all, humanists, and, in turn, the existentialist, and, in a general way, all philosophers. Nowadays, a lot of political currents are likewise taking up a humanism of sorts. All this adds up to a kind of attempt to restore a philosophy which, despite its claim, is, at bottom, unwilling to involve itself, not only from a political and social point of view, but in a profound philosophical sense as well. When Christianity claims above all to be humanistic, it is because it refuses to involve itself, because it can not involve itself; in other words it can not take part in the struggle of the progressive forces, because it is based on positions which, in regard to this revolution, are reactionary. When pseudo-Marxists or liberals cry up the dignity of the person above all else, it's because they shrink from the demands of the present world situation. Likewise, the existentialist as liberal cries up man in general because he doesn't succeed in formulating a position that events demand, and the only positive position that we know of is Marxism. It's Marxism that poses the real problems of the age.

It is not true that a man has freedom of choice in the sense that as a result of this choice he invests his activity with a meaning that it otherwise would not have. It is not enough to say that men can fight for freedom without knowing that they're fighting for freedom; or, if such be the case, what it does mean, if we give the observation its full import, is that men

can be involved in, and fight for, a cause that
dominates them, that is, they can act in a
project larger than themselves, and not only
for something which springs from themselves.
Because, in short, if a man fights for freedom
without knowing and without exactly formulating how and why he's fighting, it means that
his acts are involved in a series of consequences
which work their way into a causal network
whose ins and outs he doesn't quite grasp, but
which, all the same, embrace his action and
give it a meaning in relation to the activity of
others, not only of other men, but of the natural
environment in which men act.

But from your point of view the choice is a
pre-choice—I keep coming back to this prefix
because I think there's always a reservation
which intervenes—in this sort of pre-choice
where one is dealing with a freedom of pre-
indifference. But your notion of condition and
freedom is bound up with a definition of objects about which a word should be said. Indeed, it's from this idea of the world of objects,
of instrumentality, that you deduce everything
else. In the likeness of the discontinuous ex-

istences of beings, you draw a picture of a discontinuous world of objects from which all causality is absent, except for that peculiar sort of causal relation that instrumentality does have, something passive, incomprehensible, contemptible. Existentialist man stumbles about in a universe of instruments, of obstacles which are bound up together in any which way, which lean on one another out of a queer sort of solicitude to be of service to each other, but which are tainted with a stigma that is appalling to the idealists of would-be pure externality. A kind of instrumental yet a-causal determinism.

But where does this world, the explanation of which is, moreover, quite arbitrary, and not at all consonant with modern scientific data, begin and end. As we see it, it doesn't begin or end anywhere, because the segregation that the existentialist would like to submit it to, in regard to nature, or rather the human condition, is unreal. As we see it, there is one world, one world only; and the totality of this world, both men and things—if you insist on this distinction —can be affected, in certain variable conditions by the objective sign, the plus or minus, that you place before it. The instrumentality of the stars, of anger, of the flower? I'm not going to split hairs here. However, I do maintain that your freedom, your idealism, comes out of an arbitrary scorn for things. And yet, things are quite different from the description of them that you give. You grant that they have an existence in themselves. Well, that's something. But it's a purely privative existence, an unremitting antagonism. As you see it, the physical and biological universe is never a condition, a source of conditioning; the hard, practical meaning of this word has no more reality for you than that of cause. That's why, for the existentialist man, the objective universe is only a cause for vexation, which nothing can be done about, indifferent at heart, a perpetual state of the probable; in other words, just the contrary of what it is for Marxist materialism.

For these and other reasons, you conceive the involvement of philosophy as an arbitrary decision, a free decision as you style it. You distort even the personal history of Marx when you indicate that he elaborated a philosophy by reason of the fact that he involved it. No, involvement, or rather social and political activity, was, on the contrary, a determinant of his more general thinking. His doctrines achieved their precise statement through a multiplicity of experiences. It appears evident to me that there was a conscious connection between the development of philosophical thought in Marx, and political and social development. Moreover, that's more or less true for the earlier philosophers. If Kant is a systematic philosopher known for having kept apart from all political activity, that doesn't mean that his philosophy didn't play a certain political role. According to Heine, Kant was the German Robespierre. And insofar as it might be granted that, in the age of Descartes, for example, the development of philosophy did not play an immediate political role—which is not correct—this has become impossible since the last century. To return today, in whatever form, to a position antedating Marxism is what I call reverting to old-fashioned reformism.

Therefore, existentialism, insofar as it can

inspire men with the revolutionary spirit, must first undertake a task of self-criticism. I don't think it would do this any too willingly, but it would have to do it. Its defenders would have to pass through a crisis, a dialectic crisis, so to speak, one which would retain some positions which would still have value for its adherents.

To me this seems necessary, the more so as I've been able to observe the disturbing and clearly reactionary social conclusions that some of them draw from existentialism. One of them concluded an analysis he was writing by saying that phenomenology could perform a very specific service in the social and revolutionary sphere by providing the lower middle-class with a philosophy which would enable it to be and to become the spearhead of the international revolutionary movement. By means of the intentionality of consciousness the lower middle-class could be given a philosophy to correspond to its own way of life, to enable it to become the spearhead of the world-wide revolutionary movement. I cite this example. I could cite others of the same type to show that a number of people who are quite involved in other matters, and happen to be drawn to existentialism, evolve political theories from it which, at bottom, and I come back to what I said at the start, are theories which smack of neo-liberalism, of neo-reformism.

This is positively dangerous. What we're most interested in is, not trying to find a dialectic coherence among all the fields touched on by existentialism, but seeing the orientation of these themes which, little by little, end up, maybe reluctantly, and in relation to some inquiry, theory, or attitude that you consider very definite, in something which isn't quietism, of course—for to speak, in our age, of quietism is to stack the cards, it's something out of the question—but in something like marking time. This may not be inconsistent with certain private involvements but it is inconsistent with the quest for an involvement which calls for a collective value and, above all, for a prescriptive value. Why shouldn't existentialism give directives? In the name of freedom? But if it's a philosophy with the point of view that Sartre claims it has, it must give directions; it must,

today, tell whether one ought to join the social-
ist party, the communist party, or some other; it
must tell whether it's for the party of the work-
ing-class or the party of the lower middle-
class.

M. SARTRE:

It's rather difficult to answer you completely
because you've said a great deal. I'll try to reply
to certain points I've jotted down.

First, I think that you've taken a dogmatic
position. You've said that we were returning to
a position antedating Marxism, that we were
moving backward. I think that the thing to be
proved is that we're not taking a position that
postdates it. I don't want to go into that, but I
would like to ask you where you get such a conception of truth. You think that there are some
things that are absolutely true, for you've made
some criticisms in the name of a certainty. But
if all men are objects, as you say, where does
such a certainty come from? You've said that
man refuses to treat man as an object in the
name of human dignity. That's false. The reason is of a philosophical and logical order: if

you posit a universe of objects, truth disappears. The world of the object is the world of the probable. You ought to recognize that every theory, be it scientific or philosophic, is probable. The proof is that scientific and historical theses vary, and that they are offered in the form of hypotheses. If we granted that the world of the object, the world of the probable, is the only world, we should have no more than a world of probabilities, and, therefore, as probability must depend on a number of acquired truths, where does certainty come from?

Our subjectivism allows for certainties on the basis of which we can join you in the field of the probable and justify the dogmatism you've shown during your exposition and which is incomprehensible in the position you've taken. If you do not define truth, how is Marx's theory to be conceived otherwise than as a doctrine which appears, disappears, is modified, and has only the value of a theory? How is a dialectic of history to be established if one doesn't begin by setting up certain rules? We find them in the Cartesian *cogito*; we can find them only by placing ourselves on the grounds of subjectivity. We've never argued about the fact that man is constantly an object for man, but, reciprocally, to grasp the object as such, a subject is needed which is aware of itself as subject.

Then, you talk of a human condition which you sometimes call pre-condition, and you speak of a pre-determination. What you fail to see is that we hold to many of the descriptions given by Marxism. You can't criticize me as you criticize the people of the eighteenth century who were completely unaware of the question. What you have said about determination we have known for a long time. For us, the real problem is to define the conditions under which there is universality. Since there is no human nature, how, in a constantly changing history, do you keep enough universal principles to be able to interpret, for example, the phenomenon of Spartacus, which assumes a minimum comprehension of the period? We are in agreement on this point: there is no human nature. In other words, each age develops according to dialectical laws, and what men are depends upon the age and not on a human nature.

M. Naville:

When you try to explain something, you say "It's because we refer to a certain situation." As for us, we refer to the analogy or the differences between the social life of such and such an age compared to our own. If, on the contrary, we attempted to analyze this analogy by working with an abstraction, we'd never get anywhere. Thus, suppose that two thousand years from now someone wanted to analyze the present situation only by propositions relating to the human condition in general. How would he manage to carry on a retrospective analysis? He'd never get there.

M. Sartre:

We've never thought that it wasn't necessary to analyze human conditions or individual intentions. What we call the situation is precisely the ensemble of material and even psychoanalytical conditions which, in a given age give a specific character to an ensemble.

M. Naville:

I don't think that your definition is consistent with your texts. All the same, it does make it quite clear that your view of the situation can't be even remotely identified with a Marxist view because it denies causality. Your definition has no preciseness. Often it skips neatly from one position to another without defining them strictly enough. For us, a situation is a co-ordinated ensemble which is manifested by a whole series of determinations, a causal kind of determination, including the statistical kind of causality.

M. SARTRE:

You talk of a statistical order of causality. That doesn't mean a thing. I wish you'd tell me clearly and precisely what you mean by causality. The day a Marxist explains it to me I'll believe in Marxist causality. When someone talks to you of freedom, you go about saying, "I beg your pardon, there is causality." You're unable to give any account of this causality, which has no meaning except in Hegel. What you've got is a Marxist dream of causality.

M. NAVILLE:

Do you grant that there is a scientific truth? Possibly there are areas which aren't subject to truths of any sort. But the world of objects—you do grant that there is such a thing, I hope—is the world that the sciences are concerned with. But for you it's a world which has only probability and which doesn't attain truth. Therefore, the world of objects, which is that of science, does not admit of absolute truth. But it attains a relative truth. However, will you admit that these sciences make use of the notion of causality?

M. SARTRE:

Absolutely not. The sciences are abstract. They study the variations of equally abstract factors and not real causality. It's a matter of universal factors in a framework where the connections can be studied. Whereas in Marxism it's a matter of the examination of a unique ensemble where one is hunting for causality. It's not the same thing as scientific causality at all.

M. NAVILLE:

You spoke at some length of the case of the young man who came to see you.

M. SARTRE:

Wasn't he in a situation where he could act freely?

M. NAVILLE:

He should have been answered. I would have tried to find out what he was capable of, his age, his financial possibilities, his relations with his mother. It's possible that I would have offered a probable opinion, but I would most certainly have tried to fix on a definite point of view, which, in practice, might have turned out to be a false one, but I most certainly would have had him do something.

M. SARTRE:

If he comes to ask your advice, it's because he has already chosen his answer. I could very well have given him practical advice, but since it was freedom he was after, I wanted to let him decide. Besides, I knew what he was going to do, and that's what he did do.

INDEX